Emily Wakeling

Art and Society

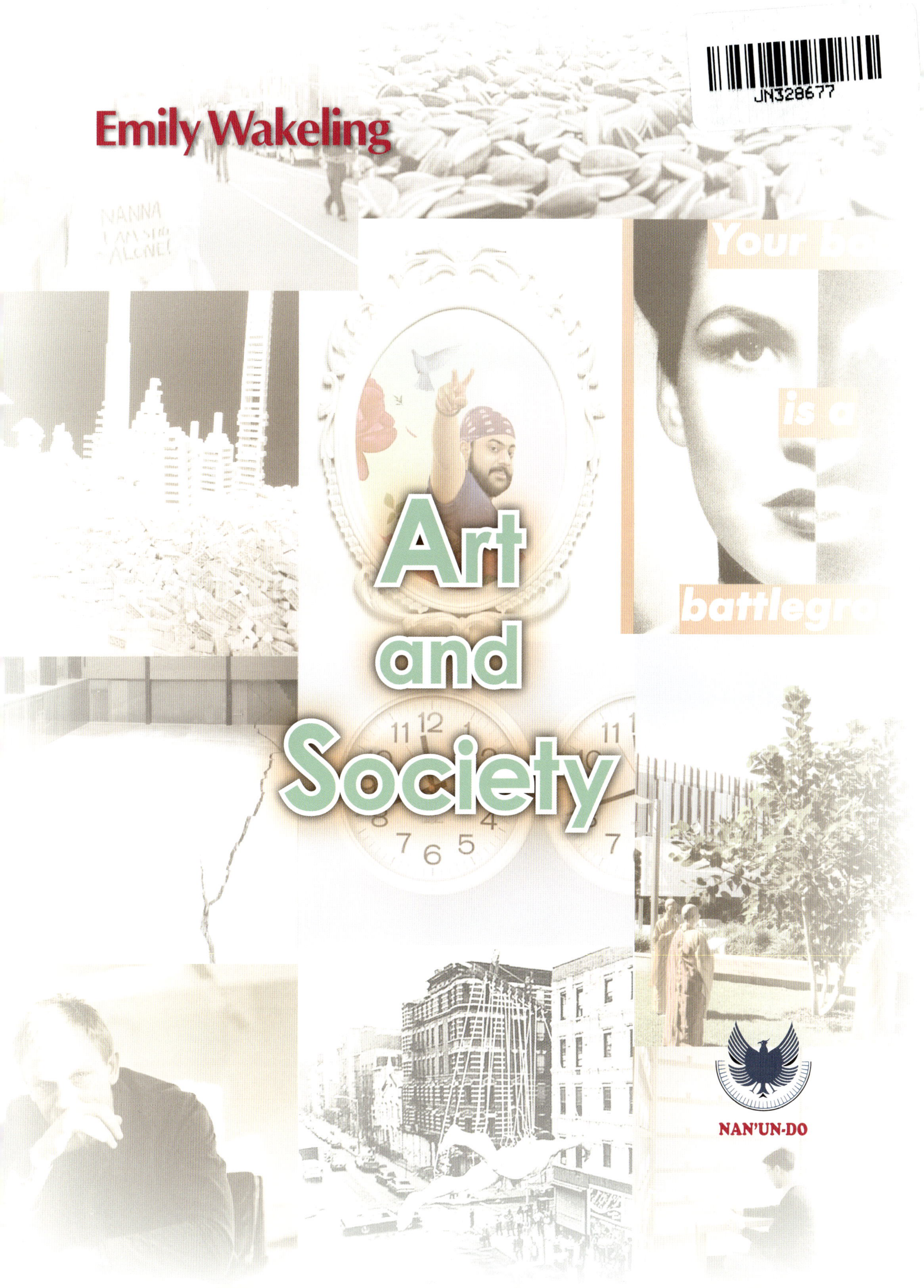

NAN'UN-DO

Acknowledgements

I wish to express my deepest thanks to Jennifer Bargewell and James Knudsen for their warm encouragement and extensive support.

Art and Society

Copyright© 2015 by Emily Wakeling

All Rights Reserved
No part of this book may be reproduced in any form without written permission from the author and Nan'un-do Co., Ltd.

このテキストの音声を無料で視聴（ストリーミング）・ダウンロードできます。自習用音声としてご活用ください。
以下のサイトにアクセスしてテキスト番号で検索してください。

https://nanun-do.com　テキスト番号 [**511672**]

※ 無線 LAN（WiFi）に接続してのご利用を推奨いたします。

※ 音声ダウンロードは Zip ファイルでの提供になります。
お使いの機器によっては別途ソフトウェア（アプリケーション）の導入が必要となります。

Art and Society 音声ダウンロードページは
左記の QR コードからもご利用になれます。

TO THE STUDENTS

Art and Society introduces you to some exciting contemporary artworks and examines the important social messages they contain. Knowing about these works of art and their themes can help us to better understand our modern, increasingly complex and globalized world. These artworks offer us a fresh and often eye-opening and controversial look at some of today's most pressing issues, including: the continuing struggle for gender equality; the effect new technology has on our humanity; the problems of living with violence and conflict; the blurred line between childhood and adulthood, and many others.

This textbook has twelve main lessons and two review lessons. Each main lesson centers around a one-page essay on an artwork and its related social issue(s) and message(s). There are five pre- and post-reading activities to help you get the most out of the essay, as well as various follow-up activities that will sharpen your writing skills, particularly those related to description and self-expression. The final activity of each lesson gives you an opportunity to describe and explain a work of art in your own words.

Working your way through this textbook will increase your understanding of contemporary society and culture. It will make you a better English speaker and writer. But the art-appreciation skills you learn along the way will also make you a more astute critic and observer. It will make your next trip to an art gallery or museum that much more enjoyable—that much more rewarding. *Art and Society* may even change the way you see the world.

CONTENTS

Lesson 1
Tradition Vs. Modernity —————— 6

Lesson 2
Migration ——————————— 12

Lesson 3
War and Conflict ——————————— 18

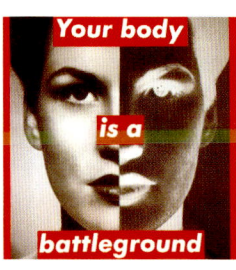

Lesson 4
Feminism ——————————— 24

Lesson 5
Queer Politics ——————————— 30

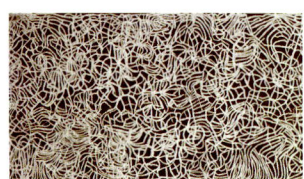

Lesson 6
Indigenous Culture in Australia —— 36

Lesson 7
Review: Lessons 1-6 ——————— 42

Lesson 8
Indigenous Culture in the Pacific —— 44

Lesson 9
Pop Culture ———————————— 50

Lesson 10
The City ——————————————— 56

Lesson 11
Youth & Adulthood ———————— 62

Lesson 12
Religion ——————————————— 68

Lesson 13
Post-humanism ——————————— 74

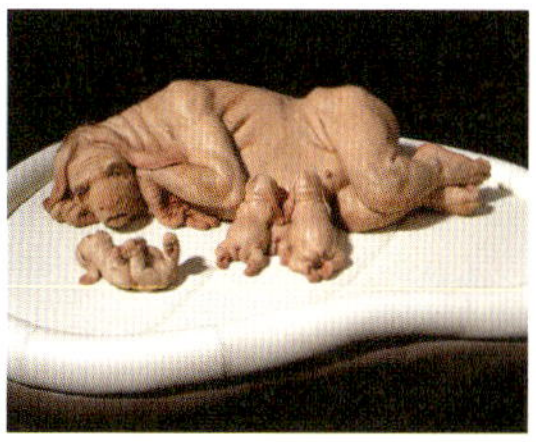

Lesson 14
Review: Lessons 8-13 ——————— 80

Lesson 1

Tradition Vs. Modernity

Ai Weiwei, *Sunflower Seeds* (2010), ceramics

Pre-reading 1:
For Thought and Discussion

1. Guess how many pieces make up this very large artwork.

2. In pairs, discuss some Japanese traditions and beliefs that still exist today. To begin, you might consider clothing, food, and holidays.

Notes:

Pre-reading 2: Art Terms and Concepts

 1-2

The paragraph below introduces some important terms and concepts that you should know about this lesson's subject. As you listen to the tape, fill in each blank with one of these words. Some words are used more than once.

| ceramic | china | kiln | pottery |
| ceramics | clay | porcelain | |

_____ is an adjective describing any object made from _____ or other non-metal materials that have been heated and then cooled. _____, with an "s," is a noun meaning _____ things _____, or the art of making such things. The word _____ has to do specifically with _____ that are only made of _____. The heating process usually involves a _____, which is an extremely hot oven designed to make soft materials like _____ become hard. _____ is a very fine and delicate type of _____ that originally came from China. Another word for _____ is _____, with a lower-case "c."

Pre-reading 3: Key Vocabulary

Scan through the essay on the next page and find the word or phrase in bold that matches each definition or synonym below. Then compare your answers with a partner's.

1. _____ things that are not real; copies
2. _____ people living today who make new art
3. _____ having the same meaning as another word
4. _____ to live at the same time or in the same place
5. _____ people with the skill to create handmade objects such as ceramics
6. _____ making goods by manual labor or machinery, especially on a large scale
7. _____ full of noise, disorder, and disturbance
8. _____ went against; did not agree
9. _____ lasting forever
10. _____ paid someone to work on a particular project

Pre-reading 4: Thinking Ahead

Read the questions below and think about them as you read the essay. Then, when you have finished reading, come back and write a brief answer to each question.

1. Who is the artist profiled in the essay? _____
2. What is the title of the artist's artwork? _____
3. When was it made? _____
4. What is the artwork about? CLUE: Look at the title of this lesson.

   "This artwork is about ..."

   _____

5. What did you find most interesting about the artwork?

   "I found it interesting that ..."

   _____
   _____

7

Lesson 1

Reading: *Read this essay carefully.*

An Ancient Art on a Massive Scale

Tradition and modernity: these two terms are usually at odds. While they may seem like opposites, in most countries tradition and modernity **co-exist**. Most societies keep some traditions among all the many changes that take place over time. Take, for example, the way Japan's highly modern cities contain skyscrapers as well as centuries-old temples. In English-speaking countries, most people say, "Bless you" when somebody sneezes simply because it has been done for centuries, even though the phrase has lost much of its meaning and most people don't know why they say it.

China, often called the "sleeping giant," is a rapidly modernizing country with an ancient past. During a **tumultuous** late-twentieth-century period known as the Cultural Revolution, China lost many of its traditions. Old ways of life—affecting education, religion, family life, farming, economics, and art—were stopped because of their "imperialist" qualities, which **contradicted** the new, modern Communist rules. Those broken links with its thousand-year-old past have changed China's society **permanently**.

This "broken link" is a theme in the works of many of today's Chinese artists. Ai Weiwei, one of China's most famous **contemporary artists** and the designer of Beijing's "bird's nest" Olympic Stadium, often makes artworks that highlight the differences between the old and new China. One of Ai's most ambitious works to date, created for London's Tate Modern, is called *Sunflower Seeds* (2010). Ai **commissioned** hundreds of local people in Jindezhen, a town in southern China famous for its traditional porcelain, to create small, seed-like shapes from clay, heat them in a kiln, and then paint them. By the end of production, Ai was able to bring approximately 100,000,000 of these handmade pieces of porcelain from China to London. The seeds covered most of the Tate's floor (over 100 meters in total length) and weighed in at about 100 tons.

In the past, porcelain was a highly valued Chinese export because Chinese **craftspeople** knew how to make it especially fine and delicate. During the 18th and 19th centuries, many European traders would sail to China to buy these artists' beautiful porcelain plates and vases. In many Westerners' minds, porcelain was **synonymous** with China. In Ai's work, the sunflower seeds were made using the same technique as in traditional ceramics. The work's incredible scale is meant to reflect the large changes that have taken place in China's export industry: from selling exquisite objects of great value in the 18th and 19th centuries to offering mass-produced, cheap **imitations** in the late 20th century and today. Each sunflower seed was carefully handmade using an age-old process. But China's current status as a **manufacturing** power and the artwork's sheer volume of pieces overwhelm the value of each seed.

Tradition Vs. Modernity

Reading Comprehension: *True or False?*

Read the sentences below and decide if they are true (T) or false (F).

1. In most societies, tradition and modernity cannot exist together. (T / F)
2. China lost many traditions during the twentieth century. (T / F)
3. Ai created millions and millions of sunflower seeds by himself. (T / F)
4. *Sunflower Seeds* was displayed in London. (T / F)
5. In the past, most of China's exported goods were cheap and mass-produced. (T / F)
6. *Sunflower Seeds* in a way shows how China's exports have changed from precious ceramics in the old days to cheap items today. (T / F)

Composition: *Vocabulary for Better Writing*

Read the explanation and follow the instructions below.

"The work's incredible scale is meant to reflect the large changes that have taken place in China's export industry …"

This use of *reflect* explains how the artwork can display (like a mirror's image) something very similar to the changes in China's export industry. First, rewrite the sentences below by substituting the correct form of *reflect* for the underlined parts. Then use *reflect* in a sentence of your own.

1. Everything she writes displays her personality.
   _____

2. Her personality is displayed in everything she writes.
   _____

3. _____
   _____

Lesson 1

Describing Works of Art

Why is description important?

Too often writers assume the reader will know exactly what they, the writers, are describing, but this can mislead or confuse readers, most of whom read to learn something new. If a writer writes, "The table looked like a regular table," each reader will have a different idea of what a "regular table" looks like. Therefore, to avoid misunderstanding, writers should be as precise and give as much detail as possible.

Description Activity 1: Skills for Better Description

The best way to create precise descriptions is to imagine that you are describing something that your reader has no idea of what it looks like. Here are some useful sentence patterns and common adjectives that will help you describe things more precisely.

- The size is (minute / tiny / small / medium-sized / large / big / tall / huge / giant).
- The shape is (round / wide / flat / circular / square / angular / pointy / rectangular / triangular / irregular / long / thin / deep / shallow / slim).
- The color is (dark / light / grey / black / white / red / brown / aqua / pink / multi-colored).
- The surface is (patterned / shiny / sparkly / dull / rough / spiky / fluffy / wet / slick / cracked / dry / plain).

Now choose an object in the classroom and try describing it to a listener who cannot see it. Use the sentence patterns above and the appropriate adjectives. Your listener should try to guess which object you are describing.

Description Activity 2: Listen and Write

Listen carefully to the tape while the speaker describes this ceramic artwork, and then answer these questions.

Vessel, Middle Jomon period (3000 – 2000 BC)

1. What did the speaker say the vase was made of?
2. How did the speaker describe the vase's shape?
3. How did the speaker describe the color?
4. How did the speaker describe the outside surface of the vase?

Notes:

10

Tradition Vs. Modernity

Description Activity 3: Paragraph Writing

Look at this lesson's featured artwork again and write a paragraph describing it. Use descriptive words and concepts you learned in this lesson.

11

Lesson 2

Migration

Thukral & Tagra, *Morpheus (Two Pigeons)* (2009), acrylic and oil on canvas

Pre-reading 1:
For Thought and Discussion

1. If you could live overseas, where would you live? Why?

2. Around the world, more and more people are migrating to new countries. In pairs, discuss some of the reasons why this is happening.

Notes:

Pre-reading 2: Art Terms and Concepts

 1-5

The paragraph below introduces some important terms and concepts that you should know about this lesson's subject. As you listen to the tape, fill in each blank with one of these words. Some words are used more than once.

| figurative | portrait | drawing | realistic | 2D | abstract |

_____ artworks, or flat images, which are made from paint or some other kind of wet substance, are generally called paintings. When the artwork has been created using dry substances like pencil or charcoal, it is called a _____. Paintings can be _____ (like real life) or _____. _____ paintings can be understood as simply paint on a flat surface—just colors and shapes with no recognizable "real" objects. On the other hand, _____ paintings have recognizable people, animals, things, and places. Paintings with figures of people are called _____ paintings. If the painting is a close-up image of a particular person, it is called a _____. Strictly speaking, a _____ takes a particular person's face as its subject. Some artworks, however, stretch the definition of what a _____ can be.

12

Pre-reading 3: Key Vocabulary

Scan through the essay on the next page and find the word or phrase in bold that matches each definition or synonym below. Then compare your answers with a partner's.

1. _____ people who are forced to leave home and move to another country because of war, famine, or other danger
2. _____ having to do with money
3. _____ to give up something in order to gain something else
4. _____ people who move from one country to live in another
5. _____ people born and living about the same time, considered as a group
6. _____ a country that has a strong economy and high standard of living
7. _____ the ability to move to a higher social status (i.e. from poor to rich)
8. _____ earthquakes, landslides, tsunami, forest fires, floods, etc.
9. _____ away; not present

Pre-reading 4: Thinking Ahead

Read the questions below and think about them as you read the essay. Then, when you have finished reading, come back and write a brief answer to each question.

1. Who is the artist profiled in the essay? _____
2. What is the title of the artist's artwork? _____
3. When was it made? _____
4. What is the artwork about? CLUE: Look at the title of this lesson.

    "This artwork is about …"

    _____

5. What did you find most interesting about the artwork?

    "I found it interesting that …"

    _____
    _____

13

Lesson 2

Reading: *Read this essay carefully.*

A New Generation Looks Skyward

Migration—moving from one country to another— is becoming an increasingly common condition. **Migrants** are crossing borders in growing numbers. The International Organization for Migration's World Migration Report of 2010 estimates the number of international migrants at 214 million. Human migration can be separated into two categories: "push" and "pull." People who move because of a "push" belong in the category of forced migration. **Natural disasters** or wars mean that they no longer have a safe home and must leave. These migrants are also known as **refugees**. Migrants in the "pull" category, on the other hand, move from their home country to a **developed country** such as the United Kingdom or United States to improve their job prospects and seek better lives.

One country with a great number of people who feel this pull factor is India. More and more young Indians, especially in the Punjab region, are getting an education that enables them to move to developed countries and work as doctors, scientists, technicians, or other well-paid professionals. The **financial** benefits don't just stop with the migrants themselves, however; many "pull" migrants also send money back home on a regular basis, helping their families gain **social mobility**. A young Punjabi migrant's success is also his or her family's success.

The Punjabi artist duo Thukral and Tagra are very aware of this growing trend among their **generation**. Their colorful installations, including paintings, wallpaper, and sculpture, are often inspired by this particular culture's desire to achieve higher social status by decorating their homes with ornate, Western-style furniture. For the "6th Asia-Pacific Triennial of Contemporary Art" held in 2009, Thukral and Tagra created an entire living space inside the art museum. In the artists' words, the work was about a "broken family" in which all the children have left the family home and moved overseas. While the house appears rich thanks to its many possessions, there are many reminders of the **absent** children in the details. In one room, a very long dining table is raised off the ground at one end, as if it were about to take off like an airplane. In another, a sideboard displays many photos of children now living overseas.

One painting included in the installation, *Morpheus (Two Pigeons)* (2009), depicts a young man walking toward the sun and turning back to wave goodbye. The pigeons refer to a Punjabi-language phrase about those who aim to migrate, while the title, *Morpheus*, refers to the ancient Greek god of dreams. In other words, this young man is realizing his dream of moving overseas. While the man in the painting appears cheerful, there is a touch of sadness to the artwork: this image is possibly the last his family will see of him before he boards the plane and flies away. All in all, the installation provides a colorful and thought-provoking picture of modern migration and the **sacrifices** of the families left behind.

Migration

Reading Comprehension: True or False?

Read the sentences below and decide if they are true (T) or false (F).

1. Migration is not so common these days as it used to be. (T / F)
2. Refugees are "pushed" to other countries to find better jobs. (T / F)
3. People who migrate are generally called migrants. (T / F)
4. Many Punjabi "pull" migrants send money home to their parents. (T / F)
5. Thukral and Tagra often create artworks that show the effects of migration on today's generation. (T / F)
6. The title, *Morpheus*, refers to the ancient Punjabi god of migration. (T / F)

Composition: Vocabulary for Better Writing

Read the explanation and follow the instructions below.

"... are often inspired by this particular culture's desire ..."

The phrase *inspired by* describes an artwork created because of some outside influence. First, rewrite the sentences below by substituting *inspired by* for the underlined parts. Make other changes where needed. Then use *inspired by* in a sentence of your own.

1. Pablo Picasso's painting *Guernica* was painted when the artist heard the story of fire bombings in a city in Spain.

   _____

2. The Japanese film *Nobody Knows* is based on a true story.

   _____

3. _____

   _____

15

Lesson 2

Description Activity 1: Skills for Better Description

Here are some sentence patterns and adjectives you can use to describe people's appearance.

His/her body shape is ...
 (round, fat, thin, slim, bony, tall, broad-shouldered, buxom, soft, etc.)

Her/his hair is ...
 (short, long, thick, fine, spiky, curly, wavy, straight, brunette, blonde, red, brown, black, etc.)

Her/his skin is ...
 (brown, dark, freckled, pale, tanned, wrinkled, smooth, rough, red, rosy-cheeked, glowing, etc.)

His/her expression is ...
 (unhappy, angry, calm, kind, friendly, warm, happy, tired, indifferent, aloof, etc.)

Her/his gaze is ...
 (deep, mysterious, curious, bored, friendly, cold, etc.)

Now try using these sentence patterns and adjectives to describe the appearance of someone you know well like a family member or friend. Work with a partner or in a small group.

Description Activity 2: Listen and Write

Listen carefully to the tape while the speaker describes this portrait, and then answer these questions.

Leonardo da Vinci, *Mona Lisa* (c.1503) oil on wood panel

1. How did the speaker say the painting was painted?
2. How did the speaker describe the subject's shape?
3. How did the speaker describe the subject's skin?
4. How did the speaker describe the subject's expression?

Notes:

16

Migration

Description Activity 3: *Paragraph Writing*

Look at this lesson's featured artwork again and write a paragraph describing it. Use descriptive words and concepts you learned in this and the previous lesson.

Lesson 3

War and Conflict

Doris Salcedo, *Shibboleth* (2007), installation

Pre-reading 1:
For Thought and Discussion

1. Is war a natural part of human nature? Will true peace ever be achieved?

2. The artist who created this artwork is from Colombia. In pairs, discuss what you know about Colombia.

Notes:

Pre-reading 2: Art Terms and Concepts

 1-8

The paragraph below introduces some important terms and concepts that you should know about this lesson's subject. As you listen to the tape, fill in each blank with one of these words. Some words are used more than once.

| installation | painting | projections | room | installed | sculpture | encounter |

An _____ is an artwork that doesn't just hang on walls or stand on the floor, but fills an entire _____. An _____ can include _____, _____, special _____, sound, and so on, arranged in a particular way to make viewers aware of the space around them as they look at the art. Some _____ art can use a whole gallery or a whole house. In one Tokyo gallery, Ernesto Neto _____ a gigantic hanging _____ that functioned as a kind of playground. Visitors were encouraged to climb up into the soft _____ and use its ropes to move around. The work, titled *Life Is a Body We Are Part Of* (2012), was a physical as well as visual _____.

18

Pre-reading 3: Key Vocabulary

Scan through the essay on the next page and find the word or phrase in bold that matches each definition or synonym below. Then compare your answers with a partner's.

1. _____ a group of families with the same language and culture
2. _____ human society with a highly developed culture
3. _____ an illegal drug made from the coca plant
4. _____ mental suffering; mourning
5. _____ empty area
6. _____ the sacred book of Christianity and Judaism
7. _____ extreme difficulty; complicatedness
8. _____ a war within a country between political groups or regions
9. _____ aims or motivations

Pre-reading 4: Thinking Ahead

Read the questions below and think about them as you read the essay. Then, when you have finished reading, come back and write a brief answer to each question.

1. Who is the artist profiled in the essay? _____
2. What is the title of the artist's artwork? _____
3. When was it made? _____
4. What is the artwork about? CLUE: Look at the title of this lesson.

    "This artwork is about …"

    _____

5. What did you find most interesting about the artwork?

    "I found it interesting that …"

    _____
    _____

19

Lesson 3

Reading: *Read this essay carefully.*

Art That Keeps Us Apart

Conflict has always been a large part of human history. Despite how far **civilization** has progressed, conflict is still with us. Two of history's most deadly wars occurred within the last one hundred years. The early 20th-century conflict in Europe, later known as World War I (1914-18), was at first called "the war to end all wars." After so much death and destruction, people thought, no country would ever wish to fight again. World War II began two decades later, this time causing even more death and destruction spread across four continents. But these two world wars also gave rise to the United Nations, an international organization that aims to keep peace among the countries of the world.

Colombia's **civil war** has been going on for many decades. It began when guerrilla groups—unofficial armies—rose up against the Colombian government. This South American nation has been torn apart by various warring groups, whose different political **agendas** now come second to the fight to control the illegal industry of growing and selling **cocaine**.

Doris Salcedo is a Colombian artist who feels deeply about the conflict that is dividing her home country. Salcedo does not focus on the political **complexity** of the situation; instead, she makes art about **grief** and loss. For the artist, these emotions are the most important arguments against war.

In the Tate Modern, the same London art museum that exhibited Ai Weiwei's *Sunflower Seeds* (2010), Salcedo installed a 167-metre crack in the concrete floor. Titled *Shibboleth* (2007), the installation stretches from one end of the hall to the other, starting as a tiny crack—as thin as a human hair—and getting bigger and bigger until viewers can peer down into deep, wide gaps in the floor.

This artwork is unique because it works in **negative space**. Instead of adding something to the art museum's vast hall, Salcedo has her viewers look at an empty hall. The title, *Shibboleth*, is a term that comes from **the Bible**. It describes a word or action that can only be said or done correctly by people from a particular **tribe**. A shibboleth is like a test to see whether a person belongs to a tribe or is an outsider. It separates friends from enemies. Salcedo's artwork represents the way in which "tribal" differences can start as small divisions but can grow into massive problems that can literally tear countries apart—as is happening in Colombia.

War and Conflict

Reading Comprehension: True or False?

Read the sentences below and decide if they are true (T) or false (F).

1. World War I was the war that finally ended all wars. (T / F)
2. The United Nations came into existence after World War II with the aim of working for peace. (T / F)
3. Colombia's warring groups are more interested in politics than cocaine. (T / F)
4. Doris Salcedo's *Shibboleth* is a long crack in the Tate Modern's floor. (T / F)
5. A shibboleth is a kind of test that decides which tribe or group people belong to. (T / F)

Composition: Vocabulary for Better Writing

Read the explanation and follow the instructions below.

> "... 'tribal' differences can start as small divisions but can grow into massive problems that can literally tear countries apart."

The adverb *literally* describes something that is actually true or not exaggerated. In this sentence, small differences among people have actually divided Colombia right down the middle, just as the crack in the Tate Modern's floor separates one side of the room from the other. First, rewrite these sentences by substituting *literally* for the underlined parts. Then use *literally* in a sentence of your own.

1. You can't take Dad to be telling the truth when he says he's tied up at work. He just means he's very busy.

   _____

   _____

2. Everyone in the audience was truly moved to tears by the actor's performance.

   _____

3. _____

   _____

21

Lesson 3

Description Activity 1: Skills for Better Description

A portrait is a picture of a particular person. When talking about a portrait, it's important to describe the subject's expression, and then, based on that expression, to guess what emotion he or she is feeling. On the left below are some descriptions of expressions that might be seen in a portrait. On the left are some emotions that the expressions show. Match the emotions with the expressions. Write the letters on the lines.

Expression   **Emotion**

1. This woman has a wrinkled forehead. She stares _____   a. confident / defiant
   out into the distance. Her mouth is closed tight,
   and she is covering her left cheek with her palm.

2. This boy has a pink face. His eyes are shut tight, _____   b. worried / concerned
   his mouth is open, and there are tears streaming
   down his face.

3. This man stares directly at the viewer. His _____   c. sad / upset
   muscles are relaxed. He is leaning against a wall
   with his arms crossed. He has a slight smile.

4. This woman has a red face. You can see her veins _____   d. angry / enraged
   sticking out. She is screaming at someone, and
   her eyes are bulging.

Description Activity 2: Listen and Write

Listen carefully to the tape while the speaker describes this installation, and then answer these questions.

Sam Taylor-Wood, *Daniel Craig*, from the series *Crying Men* (2003), photographs

1. How does the speaker describe the series of photographs?
2. How is the subject described?
3. What emotion must the subject be feeling?
4. Which adjectives does the speaker use to describe the subject's movie role?

Notes:

War and Conflict

Description Activity 3: Paragraph Writing

Look at this lesson's featured artwork again and write a paragraph describing it. Use descriptive words and concepts you learned in this and previous lessons.

Lesson 4

Feminism

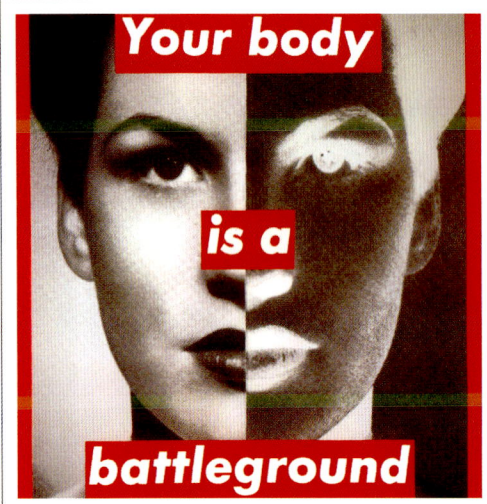

Barbara Kruger, *Untitled (Your Body is a Battleground)* (1989), poster

Pre-reading 1:
For Thought and Discussion

1. What is the purpose of advertising? Does advertising strongly influence what you buy?

2. This artwork was created for a demonstration about a certain social issue in America. In pairs, guess what the issue was.

Notes:

Pre-reading 2: Art Terms and Concepts

 1-11

The paragraph below introduces some important terms and concepts that you should know about this lesson's subject. As you listen to the tape, fill in each blank with one of these words or phrases. Some words and phrases are used more than once.

| consumers | billboards | media | brand | ads | product placement |

Advertising takes up a lot of space in modern culture. _____ dominate the visual landscape, taking many forms and using various _____. In the home, _____ names can be seen in every room. Outside the home, public spaces are filled with posters, signs, and _____. Magazines, newspapers, and the Internet are also filled with _____. In TV shows and the movies, there is a phenomenon called _____. This is when characters just "happen to" use a certain _____ of food, car, or clothing. This is no accident; it is almost always another form of advertising. In more ways than ever before, advertising aims to persuade _____ to spend money.

24

Pre-reading 3: Key Vocabulary

Scan through the essay on the next page and find the word or phrase in bold that matches each definition or synonym below. Then compare your answers with a partner's.

1. _____ the right to vote in political elections
2. _____ ideas that are taken for granted, not questioned, or tested
3. _____ the design of a text's print; typeface
4. _____ ending a pregnancy deliberately
5. _____ a social or political system led or controlled by men
6. _____ a person who creates images for advertising, magazines, etc.
7. _____ a person's social and cultural identity as male or female
8. _____ unreasonably harsh and unkind
9. _____ the ending of a marriage

Pre-reading 4: Thinking Ahead

Read the questions below and think about them as you read the essay. Then, when you have finished reading, come back and write a brief answer to each question.

1. Who is the artist profiled in the essay? _____
2. What is the title of the artist's artwork? _____
3. When was it made? _____
4. What is the artwork about? CLUE: Look at the title of this lesson.

   "This artwork is about ..."

   _____

5. What did you find most interesting about the artwork?

   "I found it interesting that ..."

   _____
   _____

25

Lesson 4

Reading: *Read this essay carefully.*

The Message is Clear

Feminism is a political movement that opposes the unfair treatment of women because of their **gender**. This unfair treatment can be found in many areas of society and culture, including employment, marriage, education, sex and reproduction, entertainment and the media, sports, and art. Violence against women and rape are its most extreme forms. In Western countries,
5 feminism has long been a force for change. It can be traced back to the **suffrage** movement of the late nineteenth century, in which many people campaigned to give women the right to vote. In the middle of the twentieth century, feminism experienced a "second wave." This was the fight to gain additional rights for women, including the right to **divorce**, the right to earn an equal salary to men, the right to equal educational opportunities, and so on.

10 Today, feminism continues to resist **patriarchy**—a male-led system of unfair laws and cultural norms that tries to keep women in an inferior social position to men. Feminism resists the patriarchal idea that women and men should look and behave a certain way simply because they were born as girls or boys. There are still many gender **assumptions**—that men are better at sports, that women are better at cooking, that men should work and women should stay at
15 home—that make it very difficult for women to freely choose to be different or to go against cultural norms.

In the 1980s, American artist Barbara Kruger worked as a **graphic designer** for women's magazines. She learned that magazine advertising is very good at sending messages to its audience and that those messages often encourage women to feel as if they should look and
20 behave in a certain way. When she left advertising and became an artist, Kruger adopted advertising techniques to make powerful messages through her art. She has a clear, simple message—don't buy into the patriarchy.

Untitled (Your body is a battleground) (1989) is one of Kruger's best-known works and exemplifies her trademark style—a white Futura **font** with red background in front of a black-
25 and-white image. In the advertising business, red is considered the most eye-catching color. Kruger's bold text in the artwork is clear and easy to read, like in an ad. It looks like a poster or billboard that could be selling something, but in fact it is a message about an important issue for many feminists. The message of the "poster," "Your body is a battleground," relates to debates surrounding **abortion**. Although abortion was made legal in the United States in the 1970s, a
30 woman's right to choose to end a pregnancy continues to be hotly contested across the nation. Kruger's message is directed to women and girls, whom she encourages to treat the issue of abortion rights like a battle against the patriarchy's **oppressive** system.

Feminism

Reading Comprehension: True or False?

Read the sentences below and decide if they are true (T) or false (F).

1. Unfair treatment of women does not relate to sports or entertainment.   (T / F)
2. Feminism in Western countries began as a campaign for women's right to vote.   (T / F)
3. Gender assumptions can limit women's freedom.   (T / F)
4. Barbara Kruger started out in magazine advertising.   (T / F)
5. Kruger's *Untitled (Your body is a battleground)* was originally an ad in a newspaper.   (T / F)
6. Abortion was made legal in the United States in the 1970s.   (T / F)

Composition: Vocabulary for Better Writing

Read the explanation and follow the instructions below.

"... Kruger adopted advertising techniques to make powerful messages through her art."

A *technique* is a special way or method to make something. It is often used in art to describe how craft or art objects are made. First, rewrite these sentences by substituting *technique* for the underlined parts. Make other changes where needed. Then use *technique* in a sentence of your own.

1. The young potter learned the method of making it from his father.

   _____

2. Yoga teaches you various ways to relax.

   _____

3. _____

   _____

27

Lesson 4

Description Activity 1: Skills for Better Description

Most of the time, we can't touch artworks when they are on display. But some special pieces, known as interactive artworks, encourage visitors to do more than just look. Below are some adjectives that describe how things feel. Write an example of something that fits each adjective.

Soft (e.g. pillow) _____
Hot _____
Fragile _____
Solid _____
Cool _____
Smooth _____
Sharp _____
Warm _____
Fluffy _____
Hollow _____
Heavy _____
Sticky _____
Rough _____
Slippery _____

Description Activity 2: Listen and Write 1-13

Listen carefully to the tape while the speaker describes this installation and then answer these questions.

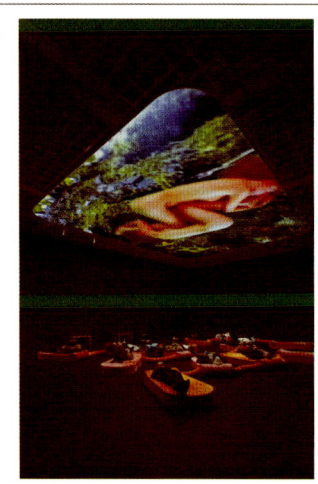

Pipilotti Rist, *Gravity Be my Friend* (2011), audio video installation

1. How does the speaker describe the mattresses?
2. In this installation, where is the video projected?
3. Where are the viewers?
4. How does the speaker describe the video?

Notes:

28

Feminism

Description Activity 3: Paragraph Writing

Look at this lesson's featured artwork again and write a paragraph describing it. Use descriptive words and concepts you learned in this and previous lessons.

Lesson 5

Queer Politics

Felix Gonzalez-Torres, *Perfect Lovers* (1991), clocks, paint on wall

Pre-reading 1:
For Thought and Discussion

1. What would perfect lovers (a couple) look and act like?
2. Do you know any influential gay or lesbian people from history or in today's world? Discuss in pairs.

Notes:

Pre-reading 2: Art Terms and Concepts

 1-14

The paragraph below introduces some important terms and concepts that you should know about this lesson's subject. As you listen to the tape, fill in each blank with one of these words. Some words are used more than once.

| skills | idea | conceptual | visual | audiences |

_____ art, also known as conceptualism, is one of the most difficult types of art for uninformed _____ to understand and appreciate. Generally speaking, _____ art considers the _____ or concept of the artwork to be more important than its _____ appearance. No traditional artistic _____ or techniques such as painting or sculpture are used in _____ art. _____ who encounter such art might see a chair set beside a photograph of a chair and accompanied by the dictionary definition of a chair, as in Joseph Kosuth's *One and Three Chairs* (1965). While the artwork's appearance may offer little _____ enjoyment, the _____ behind Kosuth's work can inspire philosophical debate about the use of language.

Pre-reading 3: Key Vocabulary

Scan through the essay on the next page and find the word or phrase in bold that matches each definition or synonym below. Then compare your answers with a partner's.

1. _____ identified an illness (usually done by a doctor)
2. _____ a group of people sharing an interest, identity, or activity
3. _____ an acronym for "acquired immune deficiency syndrome"
4. _____ recognition; tolerance; understanding
5. _____ the act of hurting others through unpleasant physical or verbal actions
6. _____ people who speak on behalf of a political or social cause
7. _____ related to feelings
8. _____ unfair treatment based on race, gender, class, etc.
9. _____ moving at exactly the same time in the same way
10. _____ used or understood by all people; general

Pre-reading 4: Thinking Ahead

Read the questions below and think about them as you read the essay. Then, when you have finished reading, come back and write a brief answer to each question.

1. Who is the artist profiled in the essay? _____
2. What is the title of the artist's artwork? _____
3. When was it made? _____
4. What is the artwork about? CLUE: Look at the title of this lesson.

   "This artwork is about …"

   _____

5. What did you find most interesting about the artwork?

   "I found it interesting that …"

   _____

   _____

Lesson 5

Reading: *Read this essay carefully.*

All You Need is Love

Over the past few decades, in many societies, there has been a rapid increase in the visibility and **acceptance** of lesbian, gay, bisexual, and transgender (LGBT) people. "Queer" is a commonly used word that describes any type of sexuality that is not "straight," or heterosexual. Originally, queer was a hateful word used to humiliate gay people, and it is still used in that context by some people. But in the 1960s and 1970s the gay **community**—the "queer" community—appropriated and re-invented the word and made it their own, taking away its hateful "sting."

Recently, political activism in the United States has helped reduce **discrimination** against gay people and has brought about the integration of same-sex relationships into society at large. In the 1970s, America's first openly gay politician, Harvey Milk, fought to stop **harassment** directed at gay people by city police. During the 1980s, however, the gay rights movement experienced a great political setback with the spread of **AIDS** and HIV. Many people in the queer community died, and misinformation about the virus caused many "straight" people to fear gay people. Today, American LGBT rights **advocates** are intensely focused on achieving equal rights in marriage and parenthood. So far, a handful of states, including New York and Washington, have changed their laws in favor of same-sex marriage, and public support is steadily growing. More and more Americans, gay or straight, are empathizing with what is at the core of the same-sex marriage campaign—the recognition of love and commitment.

The artist Felix Gonzalez-Torres was born in Cuba and lived and worked in New York City. He died of AIDS in 1996 at the age of 39. Though his works look plain and simple, they typically contain strong **emotional** messages. In this lesson's featured artwork, for example, two plain wall clocks are hanging next to each other on a pale blue wall. The title of the artwork is *Perfect Lovers* (1991), and the clocks in it are so close to each other that they are almost touching. The times on the clocks are exactly **in sync**; even the second hands move at the same time. In this sense, then, these clocks are like the perfect couple. But wall clocks are not precise measures of time. Slowly but surely, they require re-setting and go out of sync. Gonzalez-Torres made this work soon after he learned that his partner Ross had been **diagnosed** with AIDS. The clocks represent the artist's painful acknowledgment that nothing, not even or especially happiness, lasts forever. When asked to explain the artwork's light-blue background, Gonzalez-Torres said, "For me, if a beautiful memory could have a color, that color would be light blue." Gonzalez-Torres's art goes far beyond his experience of being a gay man—it is a response to **universal** experiences of love and loss.

Queer Politics

Reading Comprehension: *True or False?*

Read the sentences below and decide if they are true (T) or false (F).

1. LGBT is an acronym for lesbian, gay, bisexual, and transgender. (T / F)
2. The word "queer" is used to describe sexual relations between people of the same sex. (T / F)
3. Queer people in America are no longer hated or humiliated by straight people. (T / F)
4. More and more people in America aim to make same-sex marriage legal. (T / F)
5. Felix Gonzalez-Torres created *Perfect Lovers* when he was diagnosed with AIDS. (T / F)
6. Gonzalez-Torres used light blue in his artwork because to him it represented a beautiful memory. (T / F)

Composition: *Vocabulary for Better Writing*

Read the explanation and follow the instructions below.

"... it is still used in that <u>context</u> by some people."

An event, statement, or idea's *context* is the circumstances or situation in which it exists. First, rewrite these sentences by substituting *context* for the underlined parts. Make other changes where needed. Then use *context* in a sentence of your own.

1. Before making such a statement, you should consider the <u>atmosphere or mood</u>.

   _____

2. Was your remark made <u>to be humorous</u>, or were you being serious?

   _____

3. _____

   _____

Lesson 5

Description Activity 1: Skills for Better Description

Some art includes performance: live or recorded movement is a part of the work. Here are some adverbs and adjectives to describe performance. As you know, adjectives describe the way something looks, feels, smells, sounds, or tastes. Adverbs modify verbs to describe how an action is done. Choose the word (adjective or adverb) in the parentheses that best completes the sentence.

The performance artist walked (slow / slowly) across the stage.

She held a (tight / tightly) red cloth in her hands.

The room was (darkly / dark) and (quietly / quiet).

Her movement were (subtle / subtly).

(Sudden / Suddenly), a loud noise come from the speakers.

Description Activity 2: Listen and Write

Listen carefully to the tape while the speaker describes a performance, and then answer these questions.

Stelarc, *Street Suspension* (1984), gelatin silver photograph

1. How was the artist's body connected to the crane?
2. How does the newspaper describe the movement of the artist's body during the performance?
3. How high above the ground was the artist?
4. How long was the artist suspended?

Notes:

Queer Politics

Description Activity 3: Paragraph Writing

Look at this lesson's featured artwork again and write a paragraph describing it. Use descriptive words and concepts you learned in this and previous lessons.

35

Lesson 6

Indigenous Culture in Australia

Emily Kame Kngwarreye, *Big Yam Dreaming* (1995), acrylic paint on canvas

Pre-reading 1: *For Thought and Discussion*

1. Who were Australia's first inhabitants?
2. August 9 is International Day of the World's Indigenous Peoples. In pairs, list as many of the world's indigenous, or native, groups as you can.

Notes:

Pre-reading 2: Art Terms and Concepts

 1-17

The paragraph below introduces some important terms and concepts that you should know about this lesson's subject. As you listen to the tape, fill in each blank with one of these words. Some words are used more than once.

| sensitivity | objects | animals | content | language | symbols |

_____ are often used in art. Most of us can appreciate a beautiful painting and the skills that went into making it, but the _____ of the painting is also important. By _____ is meant the painting's images of things or people. _____, colors, plants and _____, and so on are carefully chosen because they have meanings that are connected to the artist's culture. _____ in art are not simply code signals, like traffic lights, where red means stop and green means go. Instead, they are part of a complex _____ in which green can mean jealousy or fertility or even both, depending on how the artist uses it. Moreover, the meaning of green in one culture may be different from that of another culture. It is up to each of us to explore a work of art with care and _____, and to decide for ourselves how its _____ function and what they stand for.

Pre-reading 3: Key Vocabulary

Scan through the essay on the next page and find the word or phrase in bold that matches each definition or synonym below. Then compare your answers with a partner's.

1. _____ something of importance received from the past
2. _____ people from whom you are descended
3. _____ great in size or character
4. _____ the act of killing a great number of people or animals
5. _____ a contagious disease that causes blisters and can lead to death
6. _____ having to do with something that no one else has done before
7. _____ the freedom to inhabit and use an area
8. _____ people who go to live in a new place that has few or no inhabitants
9. _____ bringing back to life
10. _____ a person who keeps something safe

Pre-reading 4: Thinking Ahead

Read the questions below and think about them as you read the essay. Then, when you have finished reading, come back and write a brief answer to each question.

1. Who is the artist profiled in the essay? _____
2. What is the title of the artist's artwork? _____
3. When was it made? _____
4. What is the artwork about? CLUE: Look at the title of this lesson.

    "This artwork is about …"

5. What did you find most interesting about the artwork?

    "I found it interesting that …"

37

Lesson 6

Reading: *Read this essay carefully.*

Ancient Dreaming Lives On

Indigenous (Aboriginal) Australians are said to have the oldest continuing culture in the world. Anthropologists estimate that some Aboriginal rock paintings in Western Australia's Pilbara region were created about 40,000 years ago. There is great diversity among Aboriginal communities, with many different customs and languages. Before the arrival of Europeans in the 18th century, approximately 250-300 different languages were spoken across the continent. Today, after two centuries of **smallpox** epidemics, **slaughter**, and the dominance of European culture, much Aboriginal culture has been lost, and only about 15 native languages are still in use. To counter this sad trend, many Indigenous Australians and their communities are **reviving** their cultural identities through contemporary art.

One of the most **pioneering** Indigenous Australian artists was Emily Kame Kngwarreye. She was born around 1910 in a place called Utopia in the desert of central Australia. Like many Aboriginal Australians, Emily was forced to work with her husband on farms owned by white **settlers** until Aboriginal **land rights** were granted, and she was able to return to live in Utopia. During the last two decades of her life, when Emily was in her 80s and 90s, she made large-scale paintings on canvas of her homeland (known to Indigenous people as "country"). Her paintings gained widespread praise, resulting in an award from the Prime Minister of Australia and some of the highest auction prices ever recorded for Australian art. After her death, Emily was honored with a large exhibition that traveled all over the world, including to Japan in 2008.

Her largest painting, *Big Yam Dreaming* (1995), is an **epic** eight meters long and three meters high. A yam is a root vegetable, found in the dry lands of Emily's "country." Above the ground, yams grow across the earth in a creeping pattern. In Emily's painting, this pattern also resembles the cracked earth on which the yam of the title grows. Incredibly, this huge painting of interconnected lines was painted in just two days—all by the artist's hands, and all spontaneously. No sketch was made beforehand, and the artist did no reworking. The black canvas was spread flat on the ground, while the artist sat and painted from around the edges. The yam was an important symbol for Emily personally. Her name, Kame, means yam flower, a name given to her because she was the **custodian** of the Anmatyerre people's traditional stories, known as "dreaming." The yam holds great importance in Emily's culture, not only because it provides food, but also because it is a symbol of her **heritage**. The plant's creeping vines connect in a complicated web that also suggests Emily's connections to her **ancestors**, whose ancient traditions are still a significant part of life in all Indigenous Australian cultures.

Indigenous Culture in Australia

Reading Comprehension: True or False?

Read the sentences below and decide if they are true (T) or false (F).

1. Indigenous Australian culture is not as old as most anthropologists think. (T / F)
2. No examples of ancient Aboriginal art remain. (T / F)
3. Much Aboriginal culture was lost because of white domination. (T / F)
4. Emily Kngwarreye was born in central Australia over 100 years ago. (T / F)
5. Emily's huge paintings of her homeland gained her an international reputation. (T / F)
6. Land rights are laws that allow Indigenous people to live on their traditional lands. (T / F)

Composition: Vocabulary for Better Writing

Read the explanation and follow the instructions below.

"In Emily's painting, this pattern also resembles the cracked earth on which the yam of the title grows."

The word *resemble* is a verb that means to look very similar to something else. First, rewrite these sentences by substituting *resemble* for the underlined parts. Make other changes where needed.

1. *The Last Samurai* was shot in New Zealand because the country's mountainous landscape looks very similar to that of Kyushu.

2. Do you think I look more like my mother or my father?

3. _____

39

Lesson 6

Description Activity 1: Skills for Better Description

Line drawings and abstract paintings can be described using the adjectives on the left below. Match the adjectives to their definitions on the right. Write the letters on the lines.

adjective		definition
1. continuous	_____	a. connecting opposite corners of a frame
2. parallel	_____	b. keeping going without a break
3. diagonal	_____	c. continuing indefinitely at the same distance apart
4. serpentine	_____	d. bending and twisting like a snake
5. wavy	_____	e. without bending or curving
6. straight	_____	f. having a series of up-and-down curves

Description Activity 2: Listen and Write

T-CD 1-19

Listen carefully to the tape while the speaker describes this painting, and then answer these questions.

1. What shape is the silkscreen print's border?
2. What did the speaker say the hand is holding?
3. What is the shape similar in size to, according to the speaker?
4. How does the speaker describe the photograph?

Notes:

Barbara Kruger, *Untitled (I shop therefore I am)* (1987), photographic silkscreen on vinyl

Indigenous Culture in Australia

Description Activity 3: *Paragraph Writing*

Look at this lesson's featured artwork again and write a paragraph describing it. Use descriptive words and concepts you learned in this and previous lessons.

Lesson 7

Look at each image below and complete the chart next to it. Write the artist's name, the title of the artwork, the year it was made, and the artistic medium it represents. Use the blank space to note down important information about the artwork's themes and the artist's artistic purpose. You may also want to include information about the artist him- or herself.

Lessons 1 Tradition Vs. Modernity	Artist: Title: Year: Medium: Notes
Lessons 2 Migration	Artist: Title: Year: Medium: Notes
Lessons 3 War and Conflict	Artist: Title: Year: Medium: Notes

Review: Lessons 1-6

Lessons 4 Feminism	Artist: Title: Year: Medium: Notes
Lessons 5 Queer Politics	Artist: Title: Year: Medium: Notes
Lessons 6 Indigenous Culture in Australia	Artist: Title: Year: Medium: Notes

Lesson 8

Indigenous Culture in the Pacific

Greg Semu, *The Last Cannibal Supper ...'Cause Tomorrow We Become Christians* (2010), photograph

Pre-reading 1:
For Thought and Discussion

1. Who were the first people in New Zealand?
2. Imagine you have been shipwrecked on a remote, Pacific island. In pairs, discuss the skills and tools you would need to survive.

Notes:

Pre-reading 2: Art Terms and Concepts

T-CD 2-1

The paragraph below introduces some important terms and concepts that you should know about this lesson's subject. As you listen to the tape, fill in each blank with one of these words. Some words are used more than once.

stored	digital	electronic	photographs	film	lens

Until the invention of _____ technology, _____ were made by exposing images on light-sensitive photographic _____. Chemical-based processing was then used to develop the image. In contrast, _____ _____ can be displayed, printed, _____, manipulated, transmitted, and archived using _____ and computer techniques. No chemical processing is required. _____ photography uses an array of _____ photodetectors to capture the image seen by the _____. The captured image is then digitized and _____ as a computer file ready for _____ processing, viewing, publishing or printing. The old process of exposing the image on photographic _____ is eliminated.

Pre-reading 3: Key Vocabulary

Scan through the essay on the next page and find the word or phrase in bold that matches each definition or synonym below. Then compare your answers with a partner's.

1. _____ easily told apart from other people or things
2. _____ the act of humans eating humans, or of an animal species eating the same species
3. _____ established political control by sending settlers to a country, region, etc.
4. _____ invention or fabrication; not facts
5. _____ overcome; took control by force
6. _____ a meal eaten late at night
7. _____ a religion based on the teachings of Jesus Christ
8. _____ followers; students
9. _____ very detailed in design or plan; having many parts

Pre-reading 4: Thinking Ahead

Read the questions below and think about them as you read the essay. Then, when you have finished reading, come back and write a brief answer to each question.

1. Who is the artist profiled in the essay? _____
2. What is the title of the artist's artwork? _____
3. When was it made? _____
4. What is the artwork about? CLUE: Look at the title of this lesson.

   "This artwork is about …"

   _____

5. What did you find most interesting about the artwork?

   "I found it interesting that …"

   _____
   _____

Lesson 8

Reading: *Read this essay carefully.*

Of Cannibals and Christians

August 9th is International Day of the World's Indigenous Peoples. As defined by the United Nations, indigenous people are the original people (or their descendants) who lived in a land before it was taken over or **conquered** by outsiders. Many indigenous peoples have maintained their traditional customs and identities with respect to food and clothing, language, use of the land and other aspects of life. This gives them a strong, deep connection with their land and their cultural heritage.

Polynesia is a large area in the southern Pacific Ocean that includes Tonga, Samoa, New Zealand, and other island nations, and stretches all the way to Hawaii and Easter Island. The region covers 112 million square kilometers. Because only a tiny fraction of this area is land surrounded by vast areas of open water, indigenous Polynesians are traditionally highly skilled sailors and navigators.

To the west of Polynesia lies Melanesia, a region that contains many countries above and to the east of Australia, including New Guinea, Fiji, New Caledonia, and the Solomon Islands. Melanesian people have **distinctive** languages and cultures that set them apart from their neighbors. Some Melanesian tribes are well known for having practiced **cannibalism**. The Kanak, for example, the local indigenous people of New Caledonia, often ate their enemies, which included some Europeans in the 19th century.

By the early 20th century, both Melanesia and Polynesia had been **colonized** by various western imperial powers. The introduction of European culture, particularly **Christianity**, quickly and permanently changed their indigenous ways of life.

Greg Semu is a Polynesian artist who creates photographs that look like paintings. Many of his artworks re-imagine the history of the colonization of various Pacific island communities. His photographs from New Caledonia are **elaborate** recreations that use the Kanak tribespeople as models. In the past, European explorers and colonizers often photographed (or painted or drew) indigenous tribes to record these peoples in their so-called "natural" state, even though that state was extinct. Semu uses photography, too, but he is aware that a photograph cannot record the whole truth. In fact, through photography, Semu creates **fiction**. The theme of *The Last Cannibal Supper ...'Cause Tomorrow We Become Christians* (2010) is not really indigenous at all, but re-tells the story from the Bible of Jesus Christ's last meal before he was crucified. Semu's artwork looks a lot like Leonardo Da Vinci's iconic *Last Supper* painting from the 15th century, but instead of showing Jesus and his **disciples**, Semu depicts a table seated with Kanak cannibals in full native dress. While Jesus died at the hands of the Romans, Semu is saying, this tribe's tradition of cannibalism died out because of the arrival of Christianity.

Indigenous Culture in the Pacific

Reading Comprehension: True or False?

Read the sentences below and decide if they are true (T) or false (F).

1. An indigenous people are defined as the original inhabitants of an area. (T / F)
2. Most Pacific Islanders have no knowledge of or connection to their cultural heritage. (T / F)
3. Polynesia is another name for Melanesia. (T / F)
4. European explorers would photograph local indigenous people in their so-called "natural" state, even though that state was extinct. (T / F)
5. Greg Semu's artworks are not photographs at all but paintings that look like photographs. (T / F)
6. *The Last Cannibal Supper ... 'Cause Tomorrow We Become Christians* retells a story from the Bible in a Pacific Island setting. (T / F)

Composition: Vocabulary for Better Writing

Read the explanation and follow the instructions below.

"His photographs from New Caledonia are elaborate recreations that use the Kanak tribespeople as models."

A *recreation* shows or creates something over again, but slightly differently. As today's essay shows, Greg Semu's artwork is a *recreation* (or re-imagining) of a painting by Leonardo Da Vinci. (Here, "recreation" is pronounced "REE-cre-Á-tion." There's another "recreation," pronounced "RÉH-cre-A-tion," that means a leisure activity. Don't confuse the two.) First, rewrite these sentences by substituting *recreation* for the underlined parts. Make other changes where needed. Then use *recreation* in a sentence of your own.

1. At Christmastime, the nativity scene (the story of the birth of Jesus Christ) is made over and over again in churches across the world.

2. Some TV news shows use actors to bring news events and stories to life.

3.

47

Lesson 8

Description Activity 1: Skills for Better Description

The composition of a 2D artwork (painting, drawing, photograph) refers to the way in which the content of the work is placed. Below are some words and phrases you can use to describe the composition of 2D artworks. Look at each image below and choose the correct word or phrase in the parentheses to complete the description.

1. The rectangular frame is a (seascape / landscape).

2. The frame is (square / rectangular / oval / circular).

3. The subject is positioned (close to / far away from) the front of the frame.

4. The main subject is positioned just off-center, with another subject (to her left behind her / to her right in front of her).

5. The horizon is positioned at the (bottom / center / top) of the frame, with the vanishing point (in the center / to the left / to the right).

6. The objects are arranged (close together / loosely) and (in / out of) balance.

Description Activity 2: Listen and Write

Listen carefully to the tape while the speaker describes this artwork, and then answer these questions.

Anastasia Klose, *Film for My Nanna* (2006), video

1. Where is the horizon positioned?
2. How does the speaker describe the arrangement of the figures in the still?
3. How is the main subject described?
4. Where are the pedestrians?

Notes:

Indigenous Culture in the Pacific

Description Activity 3: Paragraph Writing

Look at this lesson's featured artwork again and write a paragraph describing it. Use descriptive words and concepts you learned in this and previous lessons.

Lesson 9

Pop Culture

Candice Breitz, *King: A Portrait of Michael Jackson* (2005) 16-channel video installation 42:20 minutes

Pre-reading 1:
For Thought and Discussion

1. What examples of American pop culture can you see in Japan?

2. In pairs, talk about your favorite American pop stars or movie/TV stars. Explain why you like them.

Notes:

Pre-reading 2: Art Terms and Concepts

T-CD 2-4

The paragraph below introduces some important terms and concepts that you should know about this lesson's subject. As you listen to the tape, fill in each blank with one of these words. Some words are used more than once.

| film | projector | video art | digital |
| screen | movies | multi-channel | |

Moving images can be in the form of video, _____, or _____ recordings. Moving images have been used to make art for as long as moving-image technology has existed. One famous _____ is *Un Chien Andalou*, which was created by the Spanish artist Salvador Dali and the Spanish director Luis Buñuel in 1929. When hand-held video cameras became widely available in the 1960s, many more artists were able to use them to make artworks known as _____. Even today, when most moving images in art are made using digital technology, the term _____ is still used to describe any moving-image artwork. In an art gallery, _____ can be displayed in many different ways. This is what makes it different from _____, which are designed to be played only in cinemas. For example, _____ _____ uses more than one _____ or _____ at the same time. As digital technology keeps advancing, the possibilities for _____ are greatly expanding as well.

50

Pre-reading 3: Key Vocabulary

Scan through the essay on the next page and find the word or phrase in bold that matches each definition or synonym below. Then compare your answers with a partner's.

1. _____ people who dedicate themselves fully to something/someone
2. _____ the ability to judge what is good (in art, music, literature, etc.)
3. _____ to behave in an expected way or to obey a rule
4. _____ a ranking system for popular music based on record sales
5. _____ anything handed down from the past; heritage
6. _____ a division of people into different groups depending on social rank or status
7. _____ to be attractive and interesting
8. _____ faithful; devoted; firm in support of something
9. _____ used, taken in, or absorbed
10. _____ not correct; imprecise

Pre-reading 4: Thinking Ahead

Read the questions below and think about them as you read the essay. Then, when you have finished reading, come back and write a brief answer to each question.

1. Who is the artist profiled in the essay? _____
2. What is the title of the artist's artwork? _____
3. When was it made? _____
4. What is the artwork about? CLUE: Look at the title of this lesson.

    "This artwork is about …"

    _____

5. What did you find most interesting about the artwork?

    "I found it interesting that …"

    _____

51

Lesson 9

Reading: *Read this essay carefully.*

Fans Find Fame

Popular culture, or, as it is more familiarly known, pop culture, is made up of ideas, products, and images that belong to popular **taste**. Pop culture is often positioned at the "lower" end of the cultural spectrum, having less importance or value than more traditional "high-culture" art forms. This "low" ranking comes from a time in the past when **class** determined people's status in society, with popular culture seen as belonging to the "lower" classes. But these days, the influence of pop culture is so widespread that it is **inaccurate** to describe it as something **consumed** by a certain class or group of people only. Popular culture is, in fact, everyone's culture.

Pop songs are created to **appeal** to a large audience. They are often short, lively, up-tempo pieces of music that **conform** to a certain style of songwriting. Pop music is everywhere and played on all kinds of media. Even if you haven't directly consumed a song or album by purchasing a CD or MP3 file, you can listen to it indirectly on multiple formats, including advertising, television programs, and ring tones, and even in public spaces like shopping malls.

While countless musicians and performers have made it to the **pop charts**, only one has been nicknamed the "King of Pop." Michael Jackson was an American singer who found success and great fame for his catchy songs and innovative performances. As a result, the King of Pop garnered one of the largest and most devoted fan bases of any celebrity in history. To this day, his 1982 album "Thriller" remains the highest-selling album of all time, and Jackson's sound, style, and dance continue to inspire musicians of all genres.

South African artist Candice Breitz's *King: A Portrait of Michael Jackson* (2005) is a multi-channel video work that takes the pop songs of Michael Jackson as its inspiration. Sixteen **die-hard fans** were invited to listen to "Thriller" while they were being filmed by the artist. Some fans sing along in private booths, some get up and dance, and some dress up like their idol. Although Jackson's music cannot be heard in the video, anyone familiar with the songs can easily imagine them as the participants sing and move in time with the music they are listening to in their headphones.

Brietz describes her work as a portrait of the "King of Pop." The pop star himself never appears in the video, but he is represented through his music and his **loyal** followers. The video is about how every person enjoys Jackson's songs differently, and shows that a portrait of someone as famous as Michael Jackson can extend well beyond photographs and album covers. In this video portrait, Jackson is not a person—he is a pop culture **legacy** that lives on through his many fans.

Pop Culture

Reading Comprehension: True or False?

Read the sentences below and decide if they are true (T) or false (F).

1. Today, popular culture is only appreciated by a small number of people. (T / F)
2. Pop music is a part of everyday life, even if you don't buy music. (T / F)
3. Michael Jackson was also known as the "King of Pop." (T / F)
4. Michael Jackson was successful and famous for a short time, but now he is almost forgotten. (T / F)
5. Candice Breitz's portrait of Michael Jackson included actual footage of Michael performing "Thriller." (T / F)
6. Though viewers of the video can't hear the music, they can imagine it by watching the video's participants. (T / F)

Composition: Vocabulary for Better Writing

Read the explanation and follow the instructions below.

"... he is <u>represented</u> through his music and his loyal followers."

The word *represent* (here used in the past tense) means to stand in for or be present as something else. While paintings, photos, and videos can portray people, the people in them are not real. They are only *represented*. First, rewrite the sentences below by substituting *represent* for the underlined parts. Make other necessary where needed. Then use *represent* in a sentence of your own.

1. Hillary Clinton <u>stood in for</u> the United States during the United Nations meeting.

   _____

2. Each of the characters in the novel <u>symbolizes</u> one of the seven cardinal sins.

   _____

3. _____

53

Lesson 9

Description Activity 1: Skills for Better Description

To talk about artworks that feature moving images, we need to use words (adjectives) that describe the various movements. Look at the sentences below. Under "Human/Animal Movements," fill in the blank in each sentence with the name of an animal or type of person. Then choose (circle) an adjective in the parentheses that best describes it/him/her. Under "Other movements," choose an adjective in the parentheses and then fill in the blank with the name of a place/object that the adjective describes. Work with a partner.

Human/Animal Movements

1. The _____ has a/an (fast-paced / springy / ambling / tired / lumbering) walk.
2. The _____ had a/an (firm / desperate / soft / sweaty / faltering) handshake.
3. That _____ is doing a/an (energetic / graceful / awkward / silly / joyous) dance.
4. The _____ gave the crowd a/an (dramatic / confident / formal / informal / enthusiastic) wave.
5. The _____ had a/an (intense / angry / enchanted / frightening) stare.

Other Movements

6. I saw (rushing / still / swelling / fast-flowing) water in the _____.
7. I felt (strong / gale-force / icy / gentle) winds in _____.
8. I saw (gathering / still / floating) clouds in the _____.
9. I saw (blooming / wilting / drooping) flowers in the _____.
10. I saw a (speeding / swerving / rushing / stalled) car on the _____.

Description Activity 2: Listen and Write

T-CD 2-6

Listen carefully to the tape while the speaker describes this painting, and then answer these questions.

Superflex, *Flooded McDonald's* (2008), video installation, 20 minutes

1. How did the speaker describe the water?
2. What colors are mentioned?
3. According to the speaker, how do the objects float on the rising water?
4. What happens to everything at the end of the video?

Notes:

Description Activity 3: Paragraph Writing

Look at this lesson's featured artwork again and write a paragraph describing it. Use descriptive words and concepts you learned in this and previous lessons.

Lesson 10

The City

Olafur Eliasson, *Cubic Structural Evolution Project* (2004) Lego blocks

Pre-reading 1: *For Thought and Discussion*

1. Do you enjoy building things? What did you like to build when you were a child?
2. In pairs or small groups, name as many world cities as you can in two minutes.

Notes:

Pre-reading 2: Art Terms and Concepts

T-CD 2-7

The paragraph below introduces some important terms and concepts that you should know about this lesson's subject. As you listen to the tape, fill in each blank with one of these words. Some words are used more than once.

| sculptures | metal | marble | bronze | glass | mold |

Throughout much of history, _____ were like the idealized statues of human forms of ancient Greece made from _____ or _____. _____ is a type of rock that contains crystals and can come in many different colors. _____ is an alloy _____, which means that it is a mix of mostly copper and tin. _____ is heated until it is a liquid and then poured into a specially shaped _____. It then cools and hardens into the sculptor's intended shape. _____ made the ideal sculpture material because it is harder and more durable than stone or ceramics. While some contemporary artists continue to work in the grand tradition of _____ or _____ sculptures, many also create artworks using other materials. These days, _____ can be made from all kinds of materials, including wood, concrete, silicone, _____, paper, household objects, or even Lego blocks.

56

Pre-reading 3: Key Vocabulary

Scan through the essay on the next page and find the word or phrase in bold that matches each definition or synonym below. Then compare your answers with a partner's.

1. _____ having to do with a very large and densely populated city
2. _____ the mostly residential areas surrounding a city
3. _____ a work of art that invites viewers to handle or take part in it
4. _____ highly developed, especially in regard to manufacturing
5. _____ to destroy or knock down a building
6. _____ to move forward; progress
7. _____ the state of having no faults or sins; perfection
8. _____ the practice of farming; growing food or raising livestock
9. _____ having to do with waste removal and clean water

Pre-reading 4: Thinking Ahead

Read the questions below and think about them as you read the essay. Then, when you have finished reading, come back and write a brief answer to each question.

1. Who is the artist profiled in the essay? _____
2. What is the title of the artist's artwork? _____
3. When was it made? _____
4. What is the artwork about? CLUE: Look at the title of this lesson.

    "This artwork is about …"

    _____

5. What did you find most interesting about the artwork?

    "I found it interesting that …"

    _____
    _____

57

Lesson 10

Reading: Read this essay carefully.

Building Up and Down

An **industrialized**, urbanized nation is one that has a high percentage of its population living in and around major cities. In the United States, 82 percent of the population lives in cities or **suburbs**. While historically many civilizations were based on **agriculture**, today the economies of most developed nations depend on industries such as manufacturing, real estate, and
5 information technology. The world's first truly industrialized country was England. During the Industrial Revolution, important technological innovations, including the development of coal and steam power and the machines they powered, led to the rapid growth of England's economy and to cities like London, Manchester, and Leeds. Early on, houses in these cities were poorly made, cramped, and unsanitary. Later, as improvements were made to housing and **sanitation**
10 systems, and as working conditions in factories got better, most residents enjoyed a much higher standard of living.

Tokyo, when counting all of the Greater Tokyo area, is by far the most populated **metropolitan** center in the world. In the twentieth century, Tokyo suffered two major disasters. The first was the Great Kanto Earthquake of 1923. The second was the bombings by Allied forces during
15 World War II. In both disasters, over 100,000 people died, and vast sections of the city were destroyed. By 1945, about one million Tokyoites had lost their homes. But in the postwar period, thanks to Japan's strong economic growth, Tokyo was completely rebuilt and transformed. Major building and land reclamation projects led to the construction of skyscrapers, towers, highways, and airports. To this day, development steadily continues. Tokyo is a city forever changing,
20 where the old is replaced by the new practically every day.

Olafur Eliasson is a Danish artist whose **interactive artwork**, *Cubic Structural Evolution Project* (2004), is a small model city that is constantly changing. The artwork is built from Legos, the Danish toy that is used to build play-objects. Eliasson used some 400,000 white Lego blocks in this artwork, in which visitors are invited to build houses, towers, and skyscrapers to
25 add to the cityscape. Visitors are also welcome to **raze** buildings that other visitors have created and to use the "new" blocks to make new buildings. White is a color that symbolizes **purity** and cleanliness; whenever the blocks are reused, it is as though they are making a clean start. This is the evolution Eliasson refers to in his work's title: cities are always evolving. Old buildings will be destroyed, and new ones will take their place. There is an element of sadness when old
30 buildings are destroyed, especially as a result of war or natural disaster. But the artist sees this destruction as just part of the evolution of a city as it continues to **advance** towards a better version of itself.

The City

Reading Comprehension: True or False?

Read the sentences below and decide if they are true (T) or false (F).

1. Industrialized countries have most of their population living in or near cities. (T / F)

2. Tokyo experienced two major disasters in the 20th century that destroyed most of its buildings. (T / F)

3. London has passed Tokyo as the world's most populated metropolitan area. (T / F)

4. Olafur Eliasson made his artwork using a toy that was invented in his home country. (T / F)

5. Visitors can interact with Eliasson's artwork by both destroying and rebuilding it. (T / F)

6. Eliasson sees only sadness in a city's destruction. (T / F)

Composition: Vocabulary for Better Writing

Read the explanation and follow the instructions below.

"White is a color that <u>symbolizes</u> purity and cleanliness …"

As we learned earlier, a symbol is a real object that stands for or represents an idea. To *symbolize* means to use a symbol to express or represent an idea. First, rewrite these sentences by substituting *symbolize* for the underlined parts. Make other changes where needed. Then use *symbolize* in a sentence of your own.

1. Many feminists object to the use of the color pink to <u>represents</u> girls.

   _____

2. The red circle in the center of the Japanese national flag <u>stands for</u> the rising sun.

   _____

3. _____

   _____

Lesson 10

Description Activity 1: Skills for Better Description

When writing about an artwork, it is sometimes necessary or useful to describe the viewer's feelings about it. One way to describe a person's feelings is to add the suffix "-ed" to the end of some verbs. Fill in the blanks in the sentences below with the "ed" form of the verb in the parentheses.

1. The viewers were _____ by the immense size of the artwork. (to impress)
2. When the viewers got closer to the artwork, they were _____ by its hidden details. (to surprise)
3. The viewers were _____ by the artist's wry sense of humor. (to charm)
4. Some of the slow parts of the video _____ the viewers. (to bore)
5. Some of the graphic paintings of bloody battle scenes _____ visitors. (to shock)
6. Many visitors were _____ by the artwork, which had no English explanation at all. (to confuse)
7. Viewers were _____ by the fun music and cute images in the video artwork. (to entertain)
8. Visitors were _____ by the message of love of the artwork, which was dedicated to the artist's wife. (to move)

Description Activity 2: Listen and Write

T-CD 2-9

Listen carefully to the tape while the speaker describes this artwork, and then answer these questions.

Doris Salcedo, *Untitled* (1998), timber furniture, concrete

1. How did the speaker say this artwork was made?
2. How does the speaker describe the feelings of many viewers when they see this artwork?
3. How did the speaker describe the artwork's shape?
4. What does the sculpture's arrangement resemble?

Notes:

The City

Description Activity 3: Paragraph Writing

Look at this lesson's featured artwork again and write a paragraph describing it. Use descriptive words and concepts you learned in this and previous lessons.

61

Lesson 11

Youth & Adulthood

Rineke Dijkstra, *Olivier, Quartier Monclar, Djibouti, July 13, 2003* (2003), photograph.

Pre-reading 1:
For Thought and Discussion

1. How can you tell a child from a teenager? How can you tell a teenager from an adult?

2. In pairs, discuss something you used to believe as a child but don't believe now.

Notes:

Pre-reading 2: Art Terms and Concepts

T-CD 2-10

The paragraph below introduces some important terms and concepts that you should know about this lesson's subject. As you listen to the tape, fill in each blank with one of these words. Some words are used more than once.

| flattering | subject | likeness | commission | painter |

In Lesson 2, we learned that a portrait is an artwork with a close-up image of a particular person. This person is the _____ of the portrait. Traditionally, portraits were made on _____, usually paid by the _____ or by his or her rich family. Before photography, portrait paintings were the only way to visually record what a person looked like. This meant that the portrait _____ had the great responsibility of capturing a true _____ of the _____. But because the _____ was often also the buyer, the portrait had to be _____. And to be _____, sometimes the truth had to be slightly altered—as with PhotoShop today.

Pre-reading 3: Key Vocabulary

Scan through the essay on the next page and find the word or phrase in bold that matches each definition or synonym below. Then compare your answers with a partner's.

1. _____ relating to the mind
2. _____ salaried soldiers attached to special military forces
3. _____ a mark of disgrace and shame
4. _____ actions and ceremonies marking the change from childhood to adulthood
5. _____ opposite; in disagreement
6. _____ a change
7. _____ the state of expecting to give birth
8. _____ confidence; self-esteem
9. _____ so slight as to be difficult to see or notice

Pre-reading 4: Thinking Ahead

Read the questions below and think about them as you read the essay. Then, when you have finished reading, come back and write a brief answer to each question.

1. Who is the artist profiled in the essay? _____
2. What is the title of the artist's artwork? _____
3. When was it made? _____
4. What is the artwork about? CLUE: Look at the title of this lesson.

    "This artwork is about ..."

    _____

5. What did you find most interesting about the artwork?

    "I found it interesting that ..."

    _____

    _____

63

Lesson 11

Reading: *Read this essay carefully.*

When I Grow Up

When does a girl become a woman and a boy become a man? Throughout history, the dividing line between childhood and adulthood has been marked by various ceremonies and **rites of passage**. In ancient Sparta, for example, before he could be considered a man, a boy was required to go out by himself, armed with only a knife, and kill an enemy. In industrialized cultures, rites of passage are, of course, far less brutal but not as clearly recognized. Some old religious ceremonies such as Catholic "confirmation" are still held to mark the change. But often, a child is considered an adult once he or she graduates from university and joins the labor market. But what about those who don't go to university? Perhaps for them, adulthood comes with their first job; but then again, many teenagers begin working part-time jobs while still in high school or even junior high. Perhaps we could use moving out of the family home as a marker. But it is currently estimated that 85 percent of American college students move back in with their parents after graduation. So are they children again? Similarly confusing is the fact that marriage and **pregnancy**, which might be thought of as steps to adulthood, are met with scorn and social **stigma** when they are labeled "teenage marriage" or "teen pregnancy." With so many possible paths ahead of them, young people today face **conflicting** messages about the difference between youth and adulthood.

One rite of passage that can be found throughout world history is participation in war. For as long as there have been wars, there have been boys willing (or forced!) to join the fight and subsequently become recognized as men. War can also give young people an opportunity to start fresh lives. The French Foreign Legion even allows its **legionnaires** from many countries to enlist under a fake name and new nationality. For boys who wish to escape their lives and fight for a cause, the Foreign Legion provides an attractive, and usually well paid, opportunity.

The Dutch photographer Rineke Dijkstra made seven photographic portraits of Olivier Silva, a boy who joined the French Foreign Legion when he was 18 years old. The first portrait was taken just minutes after Olivier joined the elite military unit. The rest were taken over the following three years, up until the time Silva was deployed in Gabon, Africa. The final portrait is titled *Olivier, Quartier Monclar, Djibouti, July 13, 2003* (2003). "The idea was to follow a soldier, someone who comes in soft and young, then turns tough," Dijkstra explained to the *New York Times*, "but I'm really talking about a **mental** change, not a physical one." As Olivier goes through his **transition** from a new recruit to a fully trained legionnaire, the physical changes are obvious: his hair is shaved to military standard, and he is fitter and has bigger muscles. But there is a more **subtle** change that can be seen in the expression on his face: Olivier has become a man of authority and **self-assurance**.

Youth & Adulthood

Reading Comprehension: *True or False?*

Read the sentences below and decide if they are true (T) or false (F).

1. Rites of passage for boys in ancient Sparta involved proving one's courage and military skills. (T / F)
2. A child who chooses not to go to university cannot be considered on adult. (T / F)
3. Around 85 percent of American college graduates move back in with their parents after they graduate. (T / F)
4. The French Foreign Legion only accepts French boys. (T / F)
5. Olivier was sent to fight in Sierra Leone, Africa. (T / F)
6. Rineke Djikstra's photographs show Olivier's mental changes as much as his physical changes. (T / F)

Composition: *Vocabulary for Better Writing*

Read the explanation and follow the instructions below.

> "... the physical changes are obvious: his hair is shaved to military standard, and he is fitter and has bigger muscles."

The phrase *to standard* is used to show that something fits a required measurement or quality. In this case, it means to the standard (or, here, length) required by the boy's military unit. First, rewrite these sentences by substituting *to standard* for the underlined parts. Make other changes as needed. Then use *to standard* in a sentence of your own.

1. The gallery space is air-conditioned to match the required temperature of museums worldwide.

   _____
   _____

2. Do the specifications meet the customer's requirements?

   _____

3. _____
   _____

Lesson 11

Description Activity 1: Skills for Better Description

You may have seen some public artworks on the street or in town squares or plazas in your city. In pairs or in a small group, design your own public artwork. Draw it on a sheet of paper and then write a description of it using some of the adjectives and nouns below.

The size is
   (great / enormous / immense / overwhelming / towering / intimidating).

The shape is
   (triangular / rectangular / sloping / square / pointy / round / circular / oblong).

The color is
   (dark / light / shimmering / deep / rich / faded / faint / transparent / opaque).

The surface is
   (cold / cool / hot / warm / flat / concave / convex / reflective / wet / dry).

It is made from
   (concrete / steel / solid timber / plywood / cast iron / copper / bronze / fiberglass).

It is (tall / short / thick / thin / narrow / flat).

Description Activity 2: Listen and Write

T-CD 2-12

Listen carefully to the tape while the speaker describes this artwork, and then answer these questions.

Felix Gonzalez-Torres, *Untitled* (1990-91), billboard

1. How did the speaker describe the size of this artwork?
2. Where was the artwork put up?
3. How does the speaker compare the artwork to most advertising billboards?
4. Why didn't most passers-by notice the artwork?

Notes:

Youth & Adulthood

Description Activity 3: Paragraph Writing

Look at this lesson's featured artwork again and write a paragraph describing it. Use descriptive words and concepts you learned in this and previous lessons.

Lesson 12

Religion

Pre-reading 1: For Thought and Discussion

1. This tree holds great significance for a major world religion. Can you guess which one?

2. In pairs, list as many religions of the world as you can.

Notes:

Lee Mingwei, *Bodhi Tree Project* (2008), Bodhi tree, marble seats

Pre-reading 2: Art Terms and Concepts

T-CD 2-13

The paragraph below introduces some important terms and concepts that you should know about this lesson's subject. As you listen to the tape, fill in each blank with one of these words. Some words are used more than once.

| materials | set | performance | costumes | spontaneous | daring |

As we learned earlier, _____ art is art that is made not from _____ but from actions. A work of _____ art may be either scripted or unscripted, carefully planned or _____. It can be performed by the artist him or herself or by someone else. Sometimes the audience becomes involved in the _____, too. This genre became highly popular in the 1960s and 1970s when _____ art became particularly _____. Carolee Schneeman's _____, *Meat Joy* (1964), featured men and women dressed only in their underwear and crawling around on the floor and being covered in raw meat. Matthew Barney's *Cremaster Cycle* (1994-2002) combined _____ art with elaborate _____ and _____ designs to make a unique series of films.

68

Pre-reading 3: Key Vocabulary

Scan through the essay on the next page and find the word or phrase in bold that matches each definition or synonym below. Then compare your answers with a partner's.

1. _____ recovering from an illness or injury
2. _____ belief in God or other supreme being
3. _____ having high religious importance; holy
4. _____ realization or awareness of ultimate truths
5. _____ deep thinking; meditation
6. _____ becomes less and less; decreases
7. _____ having received special favors from God
8. _____ a person who leads religious ceremonies
9. _____ making someone believe something; persuading
10. _____ travels to a place of religious importance to show one's devotion

Pre-reading 4: Thinking Ahead

Read the questions below and think about them as you read the essay. Then, when you have finished reading, come back and write a brief answer to each question.

1. Who is the artist profiled in the essay? _____
2. What is the title of the artist's artwork? _____
3. When was it made? _____
4. What is the artwork about? CLUE: Look at the title of this lesson.
   "This artwork is about … "
   _____

5. What did you find most interesting about the artwork?
   "I found it interesting that … "
   _____

69

Lesson 12

Reading: *Read this essay carefully.*

The Deep Roots of Religion

For many centuries, the Christian church played a key role in the development of art in the Western world. The highest forms of painting were depictions of Biblical scenes and Christian saints. Today, many people believe that art has replaced religion. Even as the number of churchgoers **dwindles**, art museums and auction houses are booming. Although religion and contemporary art at first seem poles apart, they do share some similarities. For instance, just as churches are buildings dedicated to **faith**, museums such as the world-famous Guggenheim Museum in New York City are buildings dedicated to art. While many Christians and Muslims make **pilgrimages** to **sacred** sites, art-lovers make pilgrimages to great museums like the Louvre and Prado and to major art festivals such as the Venice Biennale. Religion offers ideas about life and death that aim to inspire thought and action—as do many contemporary works of art.

While religion's importance may be fading in the Western world, the Taiwanese-American artist Lee Mingwei understands the important role religious practices—including those of Buddhism, Daoism, and Confucianism—still play in everyday life in his birthplace, Taiwan. His installations and performances are like ceremonies related to **healing** and human connection.

In 2006, for a project sponsored by the Gallery of Modern Art in Brisbane, Australia, the artist traveled to Sri Lanka, a country that has a special place in the history of Buddhism. Tradition says that the original Buddha came to Sri Lanka from India about 2,500 years ago, bringing with him a cutting from the tree under which he had achieved **enlightenment** (known as the Sri Maha Bodhi Tree)—a tree which still grows in Sri Lanka today. Lee says his biggest challenge was **convincing** the tree's custodians that people in the West go to art museums to be enlightened, just as the Buddhist faithful go to temples. When the Buddhist **priest** placed a cutting from the tree in Lee's hands, the priest said to the tree, "You are embarking on a great adventure to an exotic land called Australia. Your duty is to grow as big and healthy as you can, so you can offer shade and protection to the animals and children there and be a focus for **contemplation**." On its arrival in Australia, the cutting was **blessed** and planted on the art museum's grounds. The *Bodhi Tree Project* (2008), as a simple tree, does indeed provide visitors with the basic human survival needs of shade and protection. As a descendant of the sacred tree of Buddhism, it also offers enlightenment. Growing on the museum grounds, the tree suggests that religion and contemporary art have a lot in common after all.

Religion

Reading Comprehension: True or False?

Read the sentences below and decide if they are true (T) or false (F).

1. The number of Westerners who go to church is growing every year. (T / F)
2. In a way, both religious people and art-lovers make pilgrimages to their sacred places. (T / F)
3. Religion is still important to the people of Taiwan, where Lee Mingwei was born. (T / F)
4. A small version of the Sri Maha Bodhi Tree now grows outside of the Guggenheim Museum in New York City. (T / F)
5. According to the essay, religion and art have no common ground and will always stay that way. (T / F)

Composition: Vocabulary for Better Writing

Read the explanation and follow the instructions below.

"Although religion and contemporary art at first seem poles apart, they do share some similarities."

The phrase *poles apart* describes opposites or things that are very different from each other—just like the North Pole and the South Pole, the two places on Earth farthest apart. First, rewrite these sentences by substituting *poles apart* for the underlined parts. Make other changes where needed. Then use *poles apart* in a sentence of your own.

1. Though it's the same game, in some ways baseball in Japan and baseball in America are very different.

   _____
   _____

2. The two sides in the negotiations are still not even close to agreeing, and agreement may never be reached.

   _____
   _____

3. _____
   _____

Lesson 12

Description Activity 1: *Skills for Better Description*

Fill in the blank in each sentence B below with the correct adjective form of the underlined word in each sentence A (the sentences are based on sentences from Lesson 10). Sentence A describes the reactions of people looking at an artwork. Sentence B describes the artwork itself.

1. A. The audience was <u>impressed</u> by the artwork's immense size.
   B. The artwork's immense size was _____.

2. A. Viewers were <u>surprised</u> by the artwork's hidden details.
   B. The artwork's hidden details were _____.

3. A. The crowd was <u>charmed</u> by the painting's humor.
   B. The crowd found the painting's humor _____.

4. A. Viewers were <u>bored</u> by some parts of the video.
   B. Some parts of the video were _____.

5. A. Some of the graphic paintings <u>shocked</u> visitors.
   B. Some of the graphic paintings were _____.

6. A. Many visitors were <u>confused</u> by the artwork.
   B. Many visitors thought the artwork _____.

7. A. Most of the visitors were <u>entertained</u> by the performance.
   B. The performance proved to be _____.

8. A. I was greatly <u>moved</u> by the artwork's message of love.
   B. The artwork's message of love was very _____.

Description Activity 2: *Listen and Write* T-CD 2-15

Listen carefully to the tape while the speaker describes this installation, and then answer these questions.

Lee Mingwei, *Letter Writing Project* (1998)

1. How is the installation described?
2. How did the speaker say visitors can interact with the artwork?
3. How did the speaker say the installation changes?
4. How does the speaker describe the messages of the letters?

Notes:

72

Description Activity 3: Paragraph Writing

Look at this lesson's featured artwork again and write a paragraph describing it. Use descriptive words and concepts you learned in this and previous lessons.

73

Lesson 13

Post-humanism

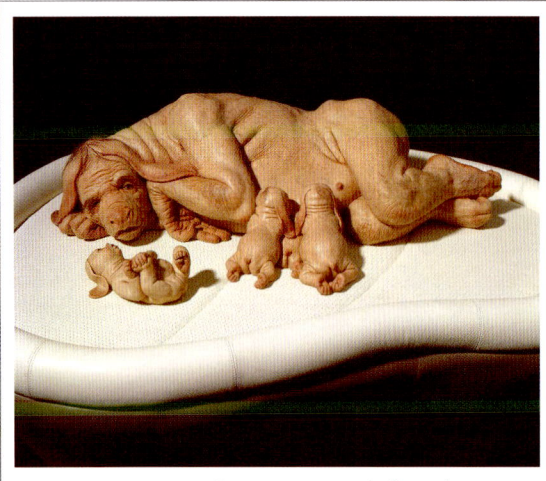

Patricia Piccinini, *The Young Family* (2002), silicone, acrylic, leather, human hair, timber

Pre-reading 1: For Thought and Discussion

1. Many movies use special effects and digital technology to create fictional creatures. Can you think of some examples?

2. What makes humans so different from other animals?

Notes:

Pre-reading 2: Art Terms and Concepts

T-CD 2-16

The paragraph below introduces some important terms and concepts that you should know about this lesson's subject. As you listen to the tape, fill in each blank with one of these words or phrases. Some words or phrases are used more than once.

| silicone | realistic | lifelike | uncanny | fiberglass | special effects |

Before the advent of photography, many artists aimed to make their paintings and sculptures look as _____ as possible. In contemporary art, _____ artworks are mostly out of favor. But a new genre, hyperrealism, is continuing the tradition of _____ art in an extreme way. Take, for example, the sculptures of Ron Mueck. Mueck creates sculptures of people that look so _____ that they are _____. Mueck picked up this skill while working for Jim Henson's studio, which is best known for the Sesame Street Muppets. He also created monsters and other _____ for various Hollywood movies. Now, instead of making Muppets and monsters, Mueck uses materials such as _____, rubber, and _____ to produce sculptures of his family that amaze viewers with their _____ accuracy.

Pre-reading 3: Key Vocabulary

Scan through the essay on the next page and find the word or phrase in bold that matches each definition or synonym below. Then compare your answers with a partner's.

1. _____ the deliberate changing of a living thing by altering its genes
2. _____ dramatic, important discoveries, usually in science or medicine
3. _____ an illness that leads to certain death
4. _____ able to exist together or get along without conflict or friction
5. _____ a part of the body (e.g. heart, liver, etc.)
6. _____ operations in which an organ is moved from one body to another
7. _____ the dead body of a person
8. _____ causing serious concern or uncomfortable feelings
9. _____ view of the future; outlook

Pre-reading 4: Thinking Ahead

Read the questions below and think about them as you read the essay. Then, when you have finished reading, come back and write a brief answer to each question.

1. Who is the artist profiled in the essay? _____
2. What is the title of the artist's artwork? _____
3. When was it made? _____
4. What is the artwork about? CLUE: Look at the title of this lesson.

    "This artwork is about ..."

    _____

5. What did you find most interesting about the artwork?

    "I found it interesting that ..."

    _____

    _____

75

Lesson 13

Reading: Read this essay carefully.

Playing God

As humanity moves further into an age of advanced medical **breakthroughs**, the question of what makes us human becomes more and more difficult to answer. Mary Shelley's classic 1818 novel, *Frankenstein*, dealt with the consequences of people's (i.e. scientists') interfering with nature and "playing God." In the novel, a scientist named Dr. Frankenstein experiments with using electricity to bring to life a human **corpse** made up of the body parts of different people. But when his experiment succeeds, he becomes deathly afraid of the hideous monster he has created. This creature, once alive, is fit to be called human, but Dr. Frankenstein cannot accept it as such, even though the monster has human feelings and suffers greatly.

In recent decades, some real-life medical breakthroughs have come close to resembling Shelley's nightmarish fiction. Today, there is a persistent shortage of **organ** donations needed to save the lives of people who have suffered a terrible accident or disease. This has led medical researchers to investigate methods for creating pigs with human genes so that body parts grown in these pigs can be transplanted into people. Animal-to-human organ **transplants** (known as xenotransplantation) have been possible since 1984, when a baby girl was given the heart of a baboon. Pig's organs are considered a more **compatible** match in size with the organs of humans, so pigs have become the focus of recent **genetic engineering** research. As scientists continue to experiment with DNA, stem cells, cloning, and prosthetic limbs, as well as to look for ways to implant various electronic gadgets under our skin, many people are looking on with concern.

Patricia Piccinini is an Australian artist who is interested in technology and medical innovation. One of her sculptures, titled *The Young Family* (2002), can be **upsetting** to look at. It should be a pleasant scene of a mother feeding her children, but instead, viewers are faced with a troubling **vision** of our possible future. At first glance, the sculpture may be mistaken for a sow and her piglets. But on closer inspection, we see that the mother's eyes are decidedly intelligent, and that instead of hoofs, she has human-like toes and toenails. Using life-like techniques similar to those used by Hollywood special effects studios, Piccinini's sculpture presents something between reality and fantasy and raises important questions about the consequences of genetic engineering for humanity. If scientists genetically alter a pig to make it more like a human, at what point might it become too human? Piccinini purposely sets this sculpture in a family setting to encourage viewers to also consider the question of love. If this were your family, would you love these babies? Moreover, if this mother could supply the organs a child of yours needed to survive a terrible **terminal disease**, would you be willing to let her or her babies die?

Post-humanism

Reading Comprehension: True or False?

Read the sentences below and decide if they are true (T) or false (F).

1. *Frankenstein* was a book about a monster called Dr. Frankenstein. (T / F)
2. Organ transplants can save the lives of people who suffer from terminal diseases or who have been in a terrible accident. (T / F)
3. Pig's body parts appear to be quite compatible with human body parts. (T / F)
4. Patricia Piccinini makes sculptures using techniques similar to Hollywood special effects studios. (T / F)
5. One question raised by *The Young Family* is what further advances in genetic engineering will eventually mean for humanity. (T / F)

Composition: Vocabulary for Better Writing

Read the explanation and follow the instructions below.

"At first glance, the sculpture may be mistaken for a sow and her piglets."

The phrase *at first glance* is used to describe how an object or scene appears before the viewer has a chance to look at or examine it closely. It implies that on closer inspection, the object or scene will look very different. First, rewrite these sentences by substituting *at first glance* for the underlined parts. Make other changes as needed. Then use *at first glance* in a sentence of your own.

1. I didn't recognize the person standing on the platform straight away. But when I looked closer, I saw that it was my friend Tomoko.

   _____

2. When you first see it, you may think this picture of a Coke can is a photograph, but it's actually a hyperrealistic painting.

   _____

3. _____

Lesson 13

Description Activity 1: Skills for Better Description

A. Similes are phrases that compare one thing to another using "as" or "like." Below are some similes commonly used in everyday English. See if you can match them. Write the words on the appropriate lines.

1. As blind as a _____.
2. As clear as _____.
3. As big as a _____.
4. As rare as _____.
5. As white as a _____.
6. As smooth as _____.
7. As cold as _____.

sheet
day
hen's teeth
silk
bat
ice
house

B. Now try making three of your own original similes by completing these sentences.

8. It was as round as _____.
9. It was as sharp as _____.
10. It was as loud as _____.

Description Activity 2: Listen and Write

T-CD 2-18

Listen carefully to the tape while the speaker describes this sculpture, and then answer these questions.

1. How does the speaker say the scooters are positioned?
2. What is the smaller scooter like?
3. What colors are used in the artwork?
4. What has the speedometer become?

Notes:

Patricia Piccinini, *Nest* (2006), fibreglass, paint, leather, steel, polycarbonate

Post-humanism

Description Activity 3: Paragraph Writing

Look at this lesson's featured artwork again and write a paragraph describing it. Use descriptive words and concepts you learned in this and previous lessons.

Lesson 14

Look at each image below and complete the chart next to it. Write the artist's name, the title of the artwork, the year it was made, and the artistic medium it represents. Use the blank space to note down important information about the artwork's themes and the artist's artistic purpose. You may also want to include information about the artist him- or herself.

Lessons 8 Indigenous Culture in the Pacific

Artist:

Title:

Year:

Medium:

Notes

_____
_____
_____
_____
_____

Lessons 9 Pop Culture

Artist:

Title:

Year:

Medium:

Notes

_____
_____
_____
_____
_____

Lessons 10 The City

Artist:

Title:

Year:

Medium:

Notes

_____
_____
_____
_____
_____

Review: Lessons 8-13

Lessons 11 Youth & Adulthood	Artist: Title: Year: Medium: Notes _____ _____ _____ _____ _____
Lessons 12 Religion	Artist: Title: Year: Medium: Notes _____ _____ _____ _____ _____
Lessons 13 Post-humanism	Artist: Title: Year: Medium: Notes _____ _____ _____ _____ _____

Biography

Emily Wakeling is a Tokyo-based lecturer, writer and curator from Brisbane, Australia. She studied at the Queensland University of Technology and earned a Masters in art history from the University of Queensland. She arrived in Tokyo in 2010 through the Monbukagakusho Graduate Research Scholarship and has settled in Japan as a freelance art writer, teacher and curator. She has written for various art journals including ArtAsiaPacific and Artforum, and teaches western culture at Kanagawa University. She has organized exhibitions of Australian artists in Tokyo galleries as well as contributing to art projects in Brisbane and Melbourne. Most recently she curated "Come Close: Japanese Artists Within their Communities" at Bus Projects, Melbourne.

Image Credit
p.23, 24, 29, 42, 43 ©Tate, London

著作権法上、無断複写・複製は禁じられています。

Art and Society	[B-782]
英語で読む『現代アートと人間社会』	

1 刷	2015年2月12日
2 刷	2021年9月10日

著 者	Emily Wakeling
発行者	南雲　一範　Kazunori Nagumo
発行所	株式会社　南雲堂 〒162-0801　東京都新宿区山吹町361 NAN'UN-DO CO., Ltd. 361 Yamabuki-cho, Shinjuku-ku, Tokyo 162-0801, Japan 振替口座：00160-0-46863 TEL：03-3268-2311（代表）／FAX：03-3269-2486 編集者　加藤　敦
組　版	柴崎　利恵
装　丁	銀月堂
検　印	省略
コード	ISBN978-4-523-17782-1　C0082

Printed in Japan

E-mail　　nanundo@post.email.ne.jp
URL　　　https://www.nanun-do.co.jp/